Here is that small print page.

Published by Sourcebooks
P.O. Box 4410, Naperville, Illinois 60567-4410
(630) 961-3900
sourcebooks.com

Follow Chippy at facebook.com/Chippythedog222
Chippy the Dog Books
Out in the Backyard
Somewhere in the U.S.A
ChippyTheDogBooks@gmail.com

Printed and bound in China.
WKT 10 9 8 7 6 5 4 3 2 1

Chippy spent a lot
of time thinking
about what he could
do to help make
you feel loved.

This is his list.

You deserve flowers every day.

3. Your Bedroom

4. Your Kitchen

5. Your Office

6. Your Bathroom

Your Neighborhood

Your Garden

Your Neighbor's Garden

The Local Park

Flower Garden

The Flower Thief

7. I'll clean up the things you drop while cooking.

8. You deserve love poems.

Ruff Ruff Bark Woofity! Bark Ruff Howlity!

I'll do all the mundane household chores.

14. If you get put on hold, hand me the phone.

Please hold. Your call is important to us.

Your call will be answered in approximately two days.

15. You'll get my help paying the bills.

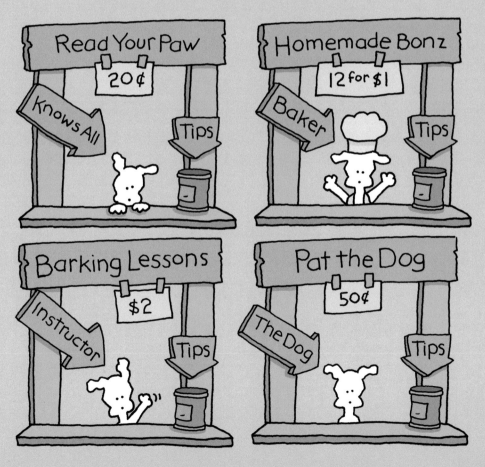

16. I would create cheesy love puns just for you.

17. I will learn to throw my voice for you.

18. You will never have to stand in line.

19. When you need a snuggle doll.

20. I'll go out for snacks when you just got to have them!

21. I'll knit cute things for you.

22.
I would happily eat everything you cook. [Even if it didn't come out too good.]

Hmm. Seems good to me.

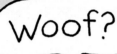
Woof?

23.
If someone you don't want to talk to calls, I will answer for you.

24.
I would create fun pictures in your hot beverages.

25. You deserve hearts!

When I travel I'll send postcards every day.

30. I will always be nice to your mom.

31. We can go on long walkies together.

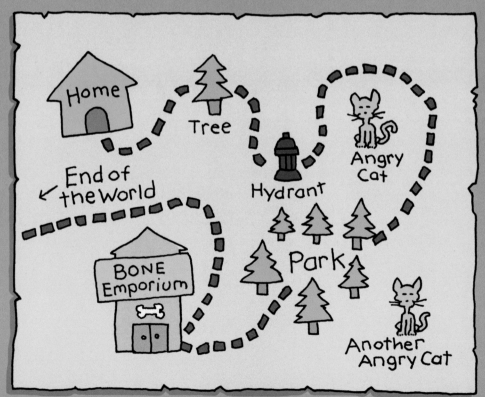

33. When you need a break from work, I will fill in for you.

Do all your paperwork.

The Bark Stops Here!

Make a bunch of copies.

We need bones.

Bring bones.

Take a lunch break.

Answer your phone.

Ruff?

34. I'll dance for you.

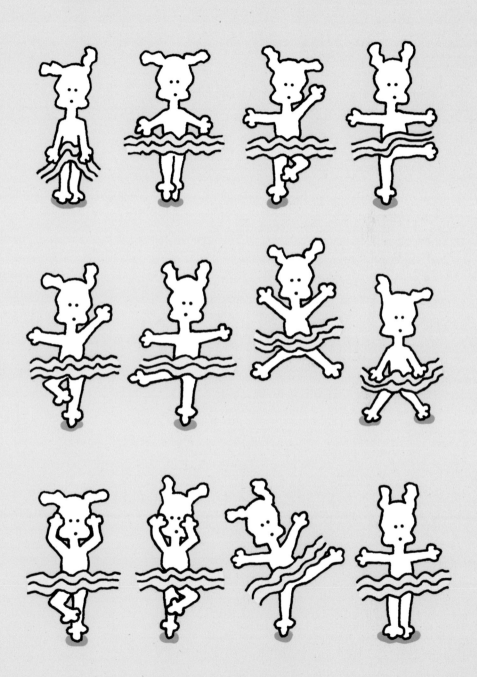

35. If for some crazy reason you want a cat, I would invite the angry cat next door over.

37. You should always have pretty curtains to look at.

38. I will make your bed every day.

39. Every dinner will be a romantic one.

Chilled Beverage

Eyes of Love

Soft Lighting

A Clean Table Cloth

Your Favorite Food

Love Songs

A Soft Comfy Seat for You

Bunny Slippers

Le Menu

40. There will always be room in my heart for you.

41. Look up in the sky!

42. All my wishes will be for your happiness.

Wishing Well

43.
I will find all your missing socks.

44. You should have puppies to play with!

45. During the day we can cloud watch together.

Reserved for you.

46. At night we can count the stars.

You will never have to worry about losing your phone.

51. I will keep strangers away from your door.

52. I will take good care of your plants when you are out of town.

53. If you get depressed I'll work to bring you back.

54. Hugs in the morning.

55. Hugs before you leave for work.

56. Hugs when you come home.

57. Hugs at night.

58. I'll help you take spontaneous selfies.

59. You should have a warm bath after a long day.

New Age Music

Scented Candles

Assorted Oils

60. Your meals should be made with love.

Doing Research

COOKBOOK

Jacques Pup-in

Menu

Doing Shopping

Doing the Cooking

Today's Menu
- Bone
- Garnish
- Water Bowl

CHIPPY

You'll hear all about my day during dinner.

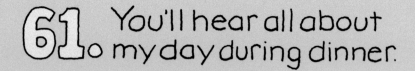

I'll keep my hair out of the sink.

63. I will take out the garbage.

I may bring back some snacks.

64. I'll take you out to that fancy restaurant you've always wanted to go to.

65. If I can't afford it, Mister Bunny will help me out.

check please.

66. I'll get that spider that was scaring you.

67. You'll always know where I am.

At your feet. In your bed. Eating dinner.

68. I will plant you a garden.

69. I'll be sure to keep sand off your towel.

70. I will carve pumpkins for you.

71. I'll shovel the walk.

72. Your closet will be arranged by color.

73. Your birthday would be the biggest holiday of the year.

A Bunch of Cards

I ♥ You!

Happy 🐝 Day!

Woof Woof Woof ♥

Mirror Ball

Happy Birthday Tree

Birthday Cake with Treats

Presents

HAPPY BIRTHDAY

Special Birthday Ribbon

All Your Favorite Songs

When you feel lonely...

78.
I'll follow you everywhere.

79.
If I couldn't be there, I would remote meet with you.

80. When you don't feel well, I'll make chicken soup.

81. Your heart will be treasured and protected.

82. You can have the remote.

83. If you want to watch scary movies, I'll try to watch too.

84. I'll watch over you while you sleep.

85. In the morning you'll get breakfast in bed.

86. Let me help you relax.

Breathe.

Relax your ears.

Relax your neck.

Relax your arms and legs.

Relax your tail.

Cuddle a dog.

When you need real passion...

El Romantico will be there!

I will always remember all the...

91. When we first met.

Kindness
Kennels

92.

My first pats.

...special moments we've shared.

93. Our first walkies.

94.
Dinnertime!

CHIPPY

95.

I'll wake up each morning happy to have another day to love you.

96.

Throughout the day, I will savor every moment together.

97.

You will be my last thought at the end of each day.

98. I'll bring you a yacht.

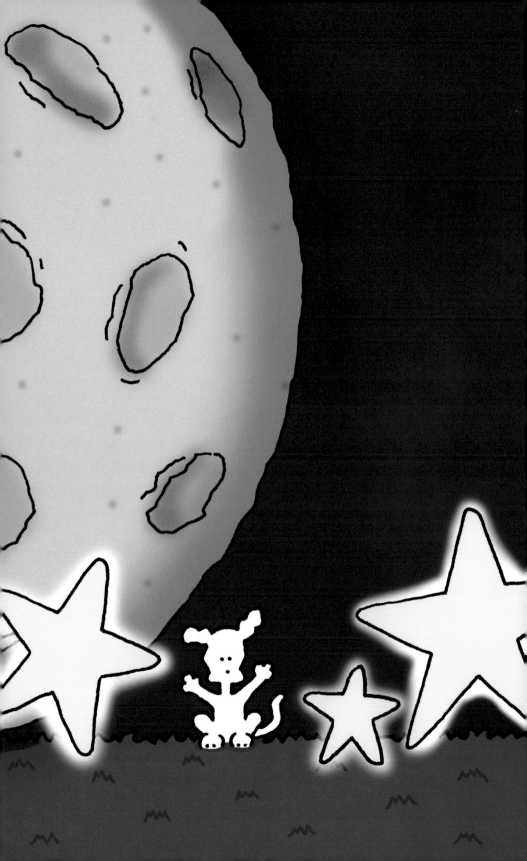

100.

And when all that is done,
I'll start a new list
for all our tomorrows
together.

Things I would NEVER do!!!

Eat your chips.

Take you for granted.

Pee on your flowers.

Use up all your
expensive moisturizers.

Ignore you.

Stop loving you.